The Nest Quest

Written by
Cath Jones

Illustrated by
Ruth Waters

Luna couldn't sleep.

It was too noisy in the nest. Mum's snoring sounded like thunder. Nana's music was too loud, and Flo and Norm would not stop fighting.

When Flo and Norm started pushing and pulling, Luna hopped out of the way.

PLOP! She fell right out of the nest!

Luna looked up at the nest. It was so high up! There was no way she could reach it on her own.

It's a bit cold down here, Luna thought. I need to look for a new nest!

She started to hop along the track, when,
SQUEAK! SQUEAK! SQUEAK!

"Come out of the cold," said a little mouse.

Luna peered into a very cosy nest. It was tucked into a hedge.

She tried to squeeze in, but there was no room for a little dragon.

"Thank you," said Luna, "but I will keep on looking."

I need to find a bigger nest, she thought.

The next nest Luna found had lots of eggs in it. It was much bigger than the mouse nest.

Luna counted sixty eggs! She squeezed in tight and lay down to sleep.

But then … **CRACK! KRICK! CRACK!** All the eggs started to hatch! Now Luna was sitting in a nest with sixty, noisy, baby ostriches.

This won't work, she thought. So she set off to look for a different nest.

Soon, Luna came to a very fine nest. It was not at all noisy, so Luna crept into it.

It was so nice and warm there that she quickly fell asleep.

But then … **CRICK! CRACK! CRUNCH!**

What a noise! thought Luna.

The eggs were starting to hatch. Luna peered at them with interest. Soft hissing sounds came from the eggs.

Goodness! thought Luna. What an odd sound.

A snake slithered out of an egg and curled itself around Luna's neck!

Luna shrieked. "Eek!"

Luna fled! She raced down the track and through a hedge. Soon, she was totally lost.

She thought about her family and their nest. It made her feel sad. Where were they?

Then Luna spotted an orangey glow. A smell of smoke drifted down from very high up.

Suddenly … "**EEK!**"

Luna was lifted right off her feet and pulled high up into the air.

It was Mum!

Mum dropped Luna right back in her nest!

"You're just in time for supper," she said.

Flo and Norm were still fighting, and Nana's music was still too loud. But it didn't matter, because Luna knew she was in the right nest.

Out in the big, wide world, there were just too many strange animals!